GHOSTMASTERS

A Chameleon Press book

GHOSTMASTERS
ISBN 978-988-18623-1-0

© 2010 Mani Rao

Published by Chameleon Press
22/F, 253-261 Hennessy Road, Hong Kong
www.chameleonpress.com

Typeset by Nicholas Gordon

First printing 2010

Artwork and photo credits
- The Ouroboros image used on the cover and in the book is courtesy Saki: *saki-blackwing.deviantart.com*
- The photograph of Mani Rao on the back cover is courtesy Tom Langdon.

GHOSTMASTERS

BY
MANI RAO

chameleon press
hong kong

Acknowledgments

The author wishes to thank the editors of publications in which the following poems previously appeared:

"θ" — *Caravan magazine* (2010) India.
"§" — *Almost Island* (2009) India.
"∞" — *Almost Island* (2009) India.
"Address" — *Quay Journal* (2006) USA.
"Airing at a sniff" — *XCP* (2007) USA. *Almost Island* (2009) India.
"Auditorium" — *Tinfish* (2008) USA.
"Bird Union" — *Kavya Bharati* (2008) India. *Softblow* (2009) Singapore.
"Calling" — *Zoland Poetry* (2007) USA. *Indian Literature* (2009) India.
"Catching up" — *91st Meridian* (2006) USA.
"Choose" originally appeared as "Testament" — *Wasafiri* (2006) UK.
"Chorus" — *91st Meridian* (2006) USA.
"Classic" — *Indian Literature* (2009) India.
"Drought" — *How2 journal* (2006).
"Ebri" — *91st Meridian* (2006) USA.
"End of Scene" — *Softblow* (2009) Singapore.
"Epitaph" — *Zoland Poetry* (2007) USA. *Chandrabhaga* (2007) India.
"Five-word poem" originally appeared as "Mutations" — *Cha* (2007) Hong Kong.
"Geocity" — *Holly Rose Review* (2010) USA.
"Grand Finale" — *Quay Journal* (2006) USA.
"Haul" — *Wasafiri* (2006) UK.
"India Song" — *PENumbra* (2006) India.
"Location" originally appeared as "En route" — *Fourth River* (2006) USA. *Chandrabhaga* (2007) India. *Asia Literary Review* (2008) Hong Kong.

"Mobius" — *Caravan magazine* (2010) India.

"Other" originally appeared as "Other Half" — *Indian Literature* (2009) India.

"Pol Pot" — *Washington Square* (2006) USA. *Asia Literary Review* (2008) Hong Kong. *Kavya Bharati* (2008) India.

"Pupa" — *Tinfish* (2008) USA.

"Re-incarnation kaleidoscope" — *Filling Station* (2006) Canada.

"Sequence" — *Papertiger 05* (2007) Australia. *Oxford Magazine* (2008) USA.

"Shorts" — *Almost Island* (2009).

"Shots" — *Softblow* (2009) Singapore.

"Slough" — *Meanjin* (2005) Australia. *The Alphabet City Trash anthology* (2006) Canada. *Asia Literary Review* (2008) Hong Kong. *Kavya Bharati* (2008) India.

"So that you know" — *Fourth River* (2006) USA. *Indian Literature* (2009) India.

"Sporous" — *Softblow* (2009) Singapore.

"Star-crossed" — *Meanjin* (2007) Australia. *Cha* (2007) Hong Kong.

"Tensile" — *Papertiger 05* (2007) Australia. *Indian Literature* (2009) India.

"Visited" — *Washington Square* (2006) USA.

"Void Plate" — Spoken-word version at *2006 New York PEN World Voices* and *Cha* (2007) Hong Kong. *Almost Island* (2009) India.

"Which way does the river flow?" — *In Posse Review, webdelsol* (2006) USA. *Asia Literary Review* (2006) Hong Kong.

"Worker" — *Tinfish* (2008) USA. *Almost Island* (2009) India.

"Writing to Stop" — *91st Meridien* (2006) USA. *Atlas* (2007) UK/India.

Contents

For your presence

So that you know

Trimming the overgrown silences of the night
Scissor beaks

It may be early unlit but the birds have begun to boil buds are
    growing wings and the tree will rise featherborne

One row of birds like a stem bipinnate will curve nicely to the breeze

One large bunch will turn like a wheel and then somersault you will
    see   a crashing tree   root fist twisting up   cumulus head rolling
    down

Blackbirds will burst a packet of tacks

A stork quadrant will appear with the mythical carpet

Chirping chandeliers will swing in from the sky in time for dusk

Classic

If everything is impermanent why do you want it

I don't want anything for ever

You will disappoint everyone
Then you will be free

Location

Hiding in a tree trunk
Looking through the hollows
Firs in new wedding gowns
Fire budding Christmas trees

It was the trees jangling interior bangles
Tigers striped past silently
Rugs on the floor of salvation wood

The first time I saw ginseng I understood body to be root
Until a slice of what I could only call steakwood

The river swears it's blue
Will carry you across

Soon as you leap in
Fast moving coils
Who said the python's dead

Where is the hatch
  Somewhere here but giant roots flowed over
Is it sealed
  Bloody me
  Will we keep

Gone too far free out at sea why does the water wave as if pining for
  the ties of Shiva's braids
The tangles at the fountainhead
From here
The view of the dance

Drought

Fruit dump under the tree
Smarting tender

Under the sore why-me look
A drool bedding noodle soup
Worm hitch

Wriggling gone from the grass no winds frisk

Collecting dry rivers
Seas

The sea was no slake
Cracked continent's crustaceous parts drifted upcreek

Said salt of the earth
Tastes like mud
Looks like chocolate

Outgrown the fish juts
Glacier not much more than a hat tipsy on a lite draught

Blood thirsty stalks faint streets

Air wavers at mouth

Toothless the well caves in

Lips do not blossom even if they meet

The speed with which air avages the plump

Yah Yah The eerious ways of god

Hot baker's fleur de mal

Catching up

The orphan and the alien met. One adopted the other.
How did they meet?
Oh in exaggerated stories always ending with a rescue and two
    foundlings.
Did you tell them they would have to forsake to save each other?
No.

Choose

They step aside letting me clean their graves
There is a pagoda in the garden where they wait talking as I mourn

I hear a voice granting me this
That I can give up my life for anyone I wish brought back to life
But only one

Father of sacrifice needs no help to draw my pity
That is piteous

Mother of passion reigned over me
I resent that

Brother of empire I would re-instate
But why

Sister of sullenness I feel for
And ignore

Lovers of the moment I cannot deny
But they did not wait for me

Children of untold stories make the most promises
They will not fulfill

Tensile

Mused at your breasts
Two at a time
Creator harvester of histories
Destroyer resident ghoul

You turn on the suck and flow but how
do you keep them away from the new one the rubbery
amniotic and chewy umbel as they loudly
gnaw and chatter how

the infant heart must be stocked with fresh f & b
and the gut
taut
clean
washed in milk

Drowning by Numbers

The retaining wall
Fell on the slope
Ran down the valley
Slipped to the beach
Dropped to sea
Laid the net
Blooming net
Closed in

We should have jacked up the foundation of our house and put back
     the map where we found it

Crusty old cat's cradle signed in blood
Engraved on leathery leaf
Our tetheredness

Fat star fell off a ring
Dotted lines re-aligned
Braying our battleship
Keeled over in a beerbottle

Down with the totem pole
Dinner at Davy Jones'

At the end it'll you and me saltface
Warm under waterquilt
Carnival of corals and fish
We'll be grateful for the fizzy water
Doe Ray Me Far Sew Lah Tea Do

Epitaph

Tooth for a tooth defang
Plucked feather mess
Ring formation around the precious gone

We the child of you and me

Two roots anchored each other
Each both tree and soil

Day and night : lips played at missing
Twilight a lasting a las t

Dyad caught in a snag
Vectors pulled
Two ends of a rope knew they were one when they tried to separate

Our future sense created a telescope
The telescope became a passage
Our passage
If it doesn't have a passage I won't call it a home

Easier to lose someone to death than to life
The present pollutes the past
The physical blocks the view
The clatter frightens the presence

When shutter sprang
We captured our stuffed animal
Stiff gloat of headstones

Horripilation on the plum tree
One sudden fruit and tiny impoverished seed inside

Those days of bottoms-up hourglass
Now the reverberations the deepwalking

We took our shoes off and walked. The fender became a reef a
    garland of shells. Crabs closed their eyes like a loud wish
    pretending to have disappeared when we went closer. I watched
    as you waited a little longer. The high tide closed in quickly
    around your feet covered the bare sand and picked up the
    backwater.

Star-crossed

You hold on to this cloud I hold on to that
Shouting the shapes over each other's voices
Everything turns to water darling
Tired
Sleep

The riddle of the moon has busted
Tell me why
Insatiable shift

Why we take to terraces gardens
Wherever we can fly silhouettes
Turning our heads slightly in love
Try on the moonring
It never fits

Your face the shadow of a witch

Sleep on the flatbed of stars
Sleep on history
Sleep in the shape of Pegasus Orion Aquila Cygnus
Heaving net
Someone always playing at Vega

Sporous

Red September path covered in kisses
Autumn abandon

Abandoning what you ask as your teeth strip and gnaw my flesh
Bruise-clouds flambéed for days
Stained as if I had gone berserk in a perfumery
Trying on too much

Address

Every evening the trees inhale birds
Swirling back home a warm shawl
But I still wait for my perch in your arms
I would peg so lightly the sheets of your night flights
We would travel in one mind your old lands my new skies
And every morning you would breathe me fly

Five-word poem

Those love cannot leave alone
Love those cannot leave alone
Cannot love leave those alone
Leave those cannot love alone
Those cannot leave love alone

End of scene

We don't see each other any more
               Was it art for art's sake
               or did we get some poems out of it

"Until part do us death"
               Until we exhaust all endings

Finally singing sol o
               Airsummons

Was supposed to give you the white kiss
               But the bloody roses
         At the lorist
               Dragons with pretty eyes

Your body suits you best
         Conducted like a plant
             All pores at once
      Posture of trunk of leaves the
        Petrifaction moment

Your uality
     iolatedness

Careful as you shape the air
Where my breasts used to be
Inhabitation's a habit

I arrive on the 18th
        eyes
        lips

2 days is what we have
        Same as 20
Spring upon your fingertips
Pert buds
Cottonwood
Bee balanced on proboscis
Uh oh in a spool
        Now the tips are green
        Now the tips are pink
        Now the tips are white

Airing at a sniff

Easy in the envelope of your hands
Rewinding to the memoir
The glyph in your graze

Rrrrrip
Rrrrrip
Rrrrrip

E a s y I said to the deaf habit of a jawdisc
What's the hurry
The season sprawls

My fiber was coarse
All five: flavor color odor vibre texture

We ran amok dusting air unsettling
And now bereft jumped on the moon
Straycow
Honeybell
What else to do but ruminate

Come graze ghost bees
About time

Grand Finale

That we are scarecrows presiding over tracts
Does not stop crows from placing feathers in our caps
And cracking up

Or stop termites pinching our feet
The powdery husk of their voices carries in the wind
Sawdust

Look there poor dog pissing in the breeze again
Chasing she who does not know fidelity

Last year's clothes are deluged by sand
In the hourglass of my body is there time
Before upside down

I've lined my pockets with the fat satin of gluttony
I've toned my thighs on charity walks
Maybe the highway robbers will have a special smile for me

Our greedy pens gorge on trees
What when we cover all the trees and nothing
Stirs the chrysalis

Re-incarnation kaleidoscope

The young wife got up
left the room and came back a dyke

The chase was abruptly called off

The child went into meditation
emerged warrior and waited
for the child-snatcher to show up again

Abra macabre
Spell it out to break the spell
Shatter light

Shots

Was in the ear foyer
Stray voice

Now sleeps on the bed
House pet

Diver followed the curve of floor
Did not see the sudden lunge

If we met now I would surely die
And I would surely if we didn't

Everywhere you are not
Your exact absence

Where does it hurt
Wingtips
Eyeballs
Lumbar
Jaw
Are you cold or hot

Suspicious at the goat's steady eyes and reminded of an early lesson
        the executor stayed his hand
If the eyes are not rolling in fear the heart may be found missing
Could be a priest in disguise

Shorts

Some deaths are well-dressed
Butterflies neatly folded

Some have banners
One ragged wing banging in the wind

One by one the petals bowed
Such polite timing
We gave each its due

Now uncapped
The smiling pod seedy teeth
The old bitter-gourd
Shaking to be a rainstick

On the contrary when
You are dying you change
To prose
The family finds out who gets what
You are finally understood

Duet

Yes we did did we
Would you could you
Oh go to bed
Sleep off
Be ok in the morning
How was it my skin
Had no buttons
Was heavy
By the fountain
Overbridge
The radio by the song
When you knew
What if
I don't come back
For a lifetime
I'll be making tea
You'll look in from the window
Over the porcelain bird
Disturb the bread and now it's flat
Next time check with me first
Drop in any time even if you are not around
You too phone when you have nothing to say

Which Way Does the River Flow?

Hilda is 80. I am 30. We are neighbors. We celebrate birthdays and we converse.

I: In Iceland they bury whales in the ground and wait for the meat to decay before eating it.
Hilda: The Chinese do the same with ham. It's good for health.
I: I'm sure it is. But there must be more to it. Art, science, for connoisseurs of decay.
Hilda: Serve it all up, maggots and all, eating carcass and maggots eating each other, with respect!

I narrate what we said.

Hilda: When I am a ghost, I will know what you get up to and all your secrets will out.
I: You'd be an old ghost, you'd be too tired.
Hilda: Ghosts drink at the fountain of youth and vitality.
I: I'd prefer if you said spirit.
Hilda: Why? Shy?
I: Because spirits go into bottles.

I hosted a masquerade on my 40th. We were in the kitchen smoking and talking. She raised a hand to her face and took off her old-bat mask. She was 70.

From that day, for every year I put on, she took off a year.

When she was sixty five I was forty five.
I gave her a goldfish tank.

Hilda: How long do they live?'

I: Ten years if taken good care of but they've been known to live 20-30 years.
Hilda: I will call the fish Tish.

I helped Hilda learn to look after Tish. Tish would do the length of the tank in twenty laps to touch the slippery wall and swim back. When the tank was cleaned, Tish stopped swimming, knocked at the glass and got lip calluses. Back from the vet, Tish demonstrated reversing powers. Hilda put an empty milk bottle in the tank. Tish drove nose in and reversed tail out. Hilda hooked out the bottle, put in a pea, put it back into the water and looked the other way. Tish went in and got the pea at once. Hilda replenished the pea several times a day and soon threw Tish and bottle out in the trash.

I was 50. She was 60.
I gave her a bouquet of roses.
Some days later I saw the stalks in the bin we shared. It crossed my mind that she had eaten the petals.

Hilda moved out of the building.
I heard she'd left me for someone younger.

Sequence

Don't keep this story to yourself

When you know the characters re-read the story

One day someone goes in search of the fictitious place in your story and
    finds it

Did you make it believe or did you not know

I got it from our dreams
When all our dreams fell in line I de-duplicated and filed them for an
    eclipse

What made a sequel necessary
To know if the story was real

When a story bewilders folding unfolding like origami   take a beaded
chain   place a scene on each bead   break the chain   swallow the beads
stand still until they settle their own sequence   collapse your intestines
take a print install in an art gallery

Slough

Nude the poet has to fashion masks out of his own diaphanous slough
Extract expressions and adore each as a face
There is no face   only a deft masker
As shadow to body   body to rhythm
Follow the ruse   this far   this guise   this guile

Slough must be eaten to the last shred
On the last journey tracks made by the head must be covered up by
    the body
Coil to the shape of a bracelet
Place tail inside mouth
Fasten clasp

The womb never leaves a child
You wear it on your back even as you look for it in absent-minded
    mourning
The new skins you grow are slough
But this is flesh – kin –
Slide back into its canoe
Bark curved from memory
And thus dressed go to the shore your bride death

37

Haul

Anchored to a sickle evergreen seacrops harvest sheaves

In the cradle of beach birthing and ghosting footprints washable ink

Dream of true nu sand unspotted by phantom gulls unraided by
    pirate crabs whereonly clawing weed and biting wind hold body
    down to lusty tide

A pendant in the clasp of extremes
Moonstone hanging on a thread
Blazing poet

The poet knows she is mere
    reflection
Stays with the metaphor
Some respectful distance from the sun

The cellist becomes a medium
Opens bodyhouse to ghostmasters who show up in the audience
They see themselves in her lake vinegar allow the gain in taste the
    seeping through the cool gauze accent

Sleeping is like fishing for myself
The old customary shoe will come along
Mermaids I didn't see myself eye
A shark scare

Then Kneejerk Stutter Piercingvision

I let the airline flow
Give myself some slack for a slow graze in the deep
Drooling all over the pin bloodshot
And reel it in

Pupa

Dreamscrawler

The first five books suck out your consciousness

Texture surfaces on your body

The dark inkwell is infested with flesh eating diamonds

Eyes at the back of the neck
Tongue jetty
Airaudience

Plenty of room on the ledge of knowing

Often in the shallows
Swollen-headed bright brim
Blinks for love in the wrong places

O for the false bottom to give

The anchor fell through the floor and staked the core
Claw marks in the unwavering sea

Worker

Pressed poet
Having to thing poems
The lights are off
Speak in your own person

Anon – Nonym – Nymous
Strong Weak Relative Nons
Us Them Impersonyms
Hate Like Ignoranymous

Many master words

Poet – pretender
Light – thunder

Permit no ambit
Even loser's glory

Humility:
Prolog's cunning
Epilog's arrogance

Stay young fox don't learn panic

That I think it is not to be feared does not mean I don't fear it. I used
    to be someone. I placed so much value on it I acted humble,
    prefacing the admission of my fortune with 'undeserved'. How
    low an opinion I had of myself that I became satisfied.

Art Artifice log away

Auditorium

Rainkiss

Some frogs gargled in the gutter
Some frog gargoyles on the path

When clouds gathered
The swelled claim – jacked-up blare –
Bellowing cars fractured in a ditch

Rumbling lawn-mower flat out finally
Good job clipper scrakes the rake

Crickets snoring in the threading salon – blunt jaw harpies – mouth
        organs – sawing machines

Clucking from a lizard poised to chirp

What ate a bird
Cat-calling from the trees

Hollow cross-hairs at the shooting range
Birds on speed

Anvil bird –
Demurrer –
Squick –

We miss

They live

Thunder, stupid
Hair-drawing
Air fell back
Void-carving
Fire sprang forward
Did anyone see the script
Those who saw were struck
Others heard about it
What did they hear
Duh
Duh
Duh

A rooster goes after the slippery sunrise with a box of crayons

Riter:
Must scratch
Pass pen please

Writing to Stop

Writers, fireflies, mistake white paper for light.

The only writing really necessary is one's Last Will and Testament and even that implies a lack of trust.

If we don't stop writing love poems, how can we be loved?

So the cured writer threw all her writing into the compost – the vegetables that grew turned eaters into writers.

Does the tree take you to the sentence or the sentence to the tree?

Writers once communed to work to take their position as gatekeepers. Now fallen asleep at the post, what's there to guard, the raided vault free of conscience, and the community's irrupted impotence pleads not guilty.

Mishearing the question – are writers profits – was a part of the symptom as writer after writer explained they were in no position to play lens. Severed, they had fallen into the pit of relativity and dedicated their lives to comparing this truth with that.

Now closed in by mirrors on all sides, there is expandable space for more writers to play the mumbling peripatetic undead, propped by a dicta-phone or notepadpen. Whatever they ear, it's not each other.

Water, flat and earless. Fins sliced before sharks tossed back into the sea.

Boiler mouth, blockaded ear valve. Mouths ladle air. Soup thinner and thinner, audience.

A matter of time before ears fall off. Meanwhile holes can be corked and lobes can be hooks.

Primitive telephones were nimble and balanced, sprinting back and forth between mouth and ear. When the handset's dumb-bell shape came about – seesaw – it was a warning, an aid to exercise both organs in equal measure. Ironically, today's bug-sized phones clog ears while really powerful microphones.

It does seem as though mouth ogre can only ever be temporarily appeased by fame's offerings, or writers who enjoy notoriety would not continue to confess. It's a getting rid of, a clean habit. According to one, there was a pile of limestone rubble in Giza after the pyramid was done. Instead of carting it all away they put it together in the shape of The Great Sphinx and gave her the job of guarding the necropolis.

Our body of writing guards our tombs and loves to strangle victims – sphingo in Greek – someone please chop her nose.
Sound continues to rise in the shape of a funnel we are digging our way out of, with.

When we have recycled the page and written on the other side of it, we wash off the ink, pulp it and make more. Consumed, our body's a matchstick in language forest fire, patches of ink fertilize the soil, new trees, more logging, more martyrs. The congenital disease, and the curse.

Can this curse be lifted.

Cure, as opposed to temporary relief from pain.

Inside the relativity pit there are those so struck, they hold language by its wings and look at it. A child's sharp delight dismembering a butterfly. Language replies, the dice is thrown, the stakes increase, both sides keep losing limbs in the fray, and the impasse is utterlessness.

Arriving here comes with a wild hope, spaceshuttles on standby, tentative about a schedule for a new watery planet. Nothing happens, language is language and gives away no clues.

When the detective hears artists are interrupted yogis she goes to Patanjali. She learns, together with the opening of certain chakra one also gains the ability to comprehend any language of any realm, animal, human or spirit. Crucially, this new skill is safest in the hands of a yogi beyond the desire to intervene. Imagine the disastrous consequences of trying to act upon overheard casual banter between idle crows. This corroborates my own childhood unbafflement with conversations between animals and humans in the Jataka tales.

Writers need help to levitate. They seem to suffocate when they don't write. Language is the air they breathe, the atmosphere they live in, and atmosphere stays bound, to the earth.

Atmosphere also holds moisture which acts like glue. Atum of Heliopolis creates son Shu the God of Air, and daughter Tefnut the Goddess of Moisture. Shu and Tefnut together procreate earth and sky. If language is Shu, Tefnut must be silence.

Silent, Charlie Chaplin and Mr.Bean become universal instead of themselves.

One, more sound. Collective flogging of sound. With everyone a mouth, speaking exercises anonymity. The cultivation of monofloral bees an impossibility as even the flowers cross-breed and defy isolation in greenhouses. Auroma no longer recognizably distinctive. Faults of the signature too inconsistent to be admissible. Chanting.

Two, more silence.

When the temperature drops suddenly, trees panic; so that they may not be stuck in the frost with their leaves out they go into hyperactivity and in a matter of hours they withdraw all the ink from their leaves, leaving behind a yellow and red dry blaze. Writer, if you want to keep that one greedy hand in the jar, godspeed pulling out in time for a sudden winter.

India Song

To the North salt mountains
To the South pepper waters
Keep ghosts out

Then who is this silent cow
Block on my narrow tar this
Late at night

White flag draped on bones
Messenger
From the recruiter

That notice nailed to her head
Two long glints in eye putty
Won't come out if I flay her

Still playing those old records
Where men slur clay
Where women trill

What is the roundabout song trying to say
For Saigal's sake

Geocity

Zero's round compound
What the zero ate was a dying periphery
Collapsed into the centre : lapsed circumference

If a line extends on its own where will it go
The purpose of a hollow : to contract
Must expand perfectly to contract perfectly
Fall out of space
Awful to be no longer ANYwhere

How to make a bird :
Take two concentric circles
Pull the inside circle out
of the outside circle
Incircle spin clockwise
Outcircle anti
Touching
Separating
Pump

Bird Union

What's your name
I asked

Omnibird
Said it in surroundsound

No primadonnas among us
One sounds like another of its kind

And doesn't mind the rhyme
It's the art of singing in a choir

Even when singing solo
Petition re petition

A signature campaign
Second sopranos

Clamoring to be first

Ebru

Up on the water   lake of oil
Up on the lake   waiting painting
A canvas lowered from the sky
To take it away in mortal colors
To air in the celestial pictures
Between eyebrows

Chorus

You are the spheres
Atmosphere

We know the nip
Your sniffer dogs

You have us hemmed in breath stitch

Stairway to Heaven

Can't see the stairway for the planet balusters
Strike them as they pass for music of the spheres

lightmeup	codechant
mockme	withmeaning
tossthis	tossthat
in	tothefire

Möbius

Glue came unstuck at horizon
We followed ourselves
Wet the sun would not light
We killed anything we did not recognize
At communion a pilgrim offered tongue for extraction
We cut a transverse section in the earth for roots found doodles
Straw went through tree trunk
Deepsea divers slipped through the tsunami fingers into its fist and
    survived
For fear of hurting maggots you used tongue not fingers to pick them
    from dog wounds
You the antelope its testy leap arching back antler bluff deliberate
    tearing of skin aroma
You tiger burning at its neck
You the ignorant
You said if I am the earth how will I bury myself
Goosebumps on surface of sea
Wind treads on water

Void Plate

When the gates of spring squeaked in the mouths of birds I put out a
    hand
Sunflower seeds embedded in my flesh
A bare-breasted mother re-filled the feeder with liquid suet
Fat River Love
Fire Forest

O the knots on Osage for fire to suckle
Sootfaced I stood uncurling fruitdrops

I could not feed the fire considering it untouchable
My only way was through it

The only way to knowledge is through God I had to say
And what   is God   she had to say

The void is the plate
Engraving zigzag
Fire the flare of sound through it
Voice ashen

Is this writing
Then where is my tongue
I've abandoned the pail and pitched my tent on seesaw water

What if I am my own witness
My ears believe each other

Other

When I draped it around myself I found it wasn't fur it was alive and
      wouldn't let go

So I danced with the bear and got to know the lightness and
      seriousness of its hands

Delicately with cultured paws it tore at my flesh and stopped   for
      some other thought

What does a half-wed do
What can a half-wed do
Keep the wound lush
Smile in secret
Stay in bed

By day freckles pop mustard seeds
By night moon glosses grain on lake rims

Calling

A fierce pea wanted to break the pan
The pan broke because the lid was shut and the fire constant
By then the pea

"Blindfolded for your own protection"

"What use if the fog clears when I won't need it"

"A blind man may see once but having seen returns to blindness. For revelations you need a seer"

Spinning the spider coagulated in the centre
Quickly everyone slung their washing over the lattice
Glory's fool began to vibrate very fast longing to be stung before his
    time

On a drip tarantic heart red rosary

Love so ft and deli (cloud blossom) it stipulates lite rolling pads of
fingers lips

Ripe pomegranate seeds in stainless peristalsis

Milking the erect nipples of god for a glass of fully-flown gold-rose
light

Oh I know you wait for me in the palace
But I am busy with the garden roses
Dazed fiery I take to their cool nectar pastures
Forgetful of the closing skies

Break my wrists and snap my knuckles so
my leaves cheer in the wind though
my body's rooted

Did I ask for a red carpet that you walk into a plantation and tenderly sparing the roses pluck all the thorns to lay upon my walkways

One of my oars was not far enough
The other a stick to stir with

A ghost ark drew up
A hitchhiking tree waved two bare arms above the deluge

The current
The opening softening wood of my body

As though I have been transplanted in deeper soil
Now the faces do not float past in my dreams
They stay shivering on my skin

I whose legs were in a knot over the title of the dance

Spine recurved into a bow almost humble
Voice jumping to be bowstring
My weight just before you raise me to your arm's taut radius
Shuddering like the bow of a ship ready
At the thought of what you aim me at I nearly swoon
And stay awake to a hissing twisting knifewedge wind

Visited

While brick wall marched shouldershoulder lapellapel and pavement
        continued brisk uniform

I was all soul that day
Knot walking
S o s l o w

The pressing wait of articulations at walled air filo
Ohm climbing to a godwashed bone-coraled emusculated standee

Took place among the trees
Heart came loose CLANG CLANG CLANG CLANG
Blood went long streamers

We trees   fountains

Pol Pot

Piece by piece clothes fell skin peeled and flesh ran in lumps and
gravy

Her sidelong glance still tosses lazily on your hammock smile
Icecube swirling provocation in your glass

The bones are good to drum with
Tusk plucked and thrown like a gauntlet
Row of ivory pawns
Pillars in war of no ceiling

You relieve the palms of superfluous arms and use their sawtooth
blades to slice our necks

Shells of infant heads you smash on trees
Oil stains trunks as tears of elephants

We play calm host to your furrowing worms
Rats tentative in our gullies
Radio flies

When you tap for one last formal dance we show up in crossbone
bowties
Jiggling our hips we make the ratatat.tat of castanets

Your raised leg swings the ball of your foot bounces tilting the earth
      the heel falls correcting the tilt
Chandeliers heave
Marbles Rrrrrr

Our skulls your lost beachballs
Somedaysome snake our scarf or rag will loop through our sockets to
      polish us

§

As soon as you start to read my poem I start to feel fond about you

Do you believe in love

the small l
those little fires
                        much huddling

two tossed aquariums in the ocean

Love | lies

                        All | lies

Outside The Aviary
Two Freewheeling Snowplumes
Interlocked
Coi !
Ploded Verges
Flurry In The Cages
The Sky Separated In To Two
The Nets High   Humane

Across The Room. Hair Moon Clouds. Smile Said Between
You And I. Sudden Gun And Shot. Eyes Jumped Water. Why
The Sidelong Glance. A Line Between Mountain And Ground.
The Range Watched. Grew. Not The Size The Lightness. Not
The Lightness The Shapeliness. Not The Shapeliness The
Sharpness. Not Of A Rumble. Of A Sesame Seed. Itch Around
Which Forms Grain. Need Wind Not Water. Light Sway.
Upward Stroke. Eye Open Dumbell.

Two Rings. Mortal § Immortal. Soft Flame. Fingernail Size.

θ

Om is a SuperConstellation
Water Sticks Together
Pain is a Verb
Death is Not
Wrong is a Place
Love has No Opposite
Perfection is a Being
A Dream with more pixels stays longer in the Memory
If there was no Fear there would be no Objects
To be Blessed Sneeze

There is knowledge and there is the memory of that knowledge by
    which we continue to regard as true what we have known to be
    true

The dewdrop knows how to roll on a razor's edge but sometimes a
    false step

She was looking for provenance to my words as if it would help her
    decide if I –
I shrieked – Nuts! They're Free, Fell From A Tree

Some
aliens
will eat
flesh
in the hope of becoming flesh

This is a chair
You may as well
sit on it
It's no good
as firewood

∞

Flashfires
Not much writing
Greek plays – accounts of murders done off stage
Why I find toes weird   because I don't use them
Why I fish without bait   because I love jaws

Heart's enlarged
Do I have to have it out
The having to honor what
means nothing but what
not honoring does not mean

Triumph threw me
Out on my ass

Ears blown
Lay throbbing

Tumortime
∞ I was supposed to swallow

Wait for the webs
Maggotflowers

Gratitude for the gone
Unsummonability

Other books by Mani Rao

Mani Rao:100 Poems (Selected Poems 1985-2005)
        Chameleon Press, Hong Kong 2003
Echolocation. Chameleon Press, Hong Kong 2003
Salt. Asia 2000, Hong Kong 2000
The Last Beach. Asia 2000, Hong Kong1999
Living Shadows. Hong Kong 1997
Catapult Season. Calcutta: Writers Workshop, 1993
Wing Span. Calcutta: Writers Workshop, 1987

www.manirao.com

CPSIA information can be obtained at www.ICGtesting.com
Printed in the USA
BVOW010415311012

304240BV00007B/33/P